EMMANUEL JOSEPH

The Silent Architects, How Billionaires Shape Industries, Redraw Maps, and Rewrite History

Copyright © 2025 by Emmanuel Joseph

All rights reserved. No part of this publication may be reproduced, stored or transmitted in any form or by any means, electronic, mechanical, photocopying, recording, scanning, or otherwise without written permission from the publisher. It is illegal to copy this book, post it to a website, or distribute it by any other means without permission.

First edition

This book was professionally typeset on Reedsy.
Find out more at reedsy.com

Contents

1	Chapter 1: The Rise of Modern Billionaires	1
2	Chapter 2: The Power of Innovation	3
3	Chapter 3: Market Disruptors	5
4	Chapter 4: Strategic Philanthropy	7
5	Chapter 5: Media Moguls and Influence	9
6	Chapter 6: Financial Titans	11
7	Chapter 7: The Real Estate Emperors	13
8	Chapter 8: Political Power Players	15
9	Chapter 9: Global Expansion	17
10	Chapter 10: Tech Giants and the Future	19

1

Chapter 1: The Rise of Modern Billionaires

The rise of modern billionaires can be traced back to the industrial age, where the seeds of immense wealth were first sown. The 19th century witnessed the emergence of industrial tycoons like Andrew Carnegie and John D. Rockefeller, who amassed fortunes through steel and oil, respectively. These pioneers laid the foundation for today's billionaires by demonstrating the power of innovation and strategic business practices. Their legacies continue to influence the way wealth is created and managed in the contemporary world.

As we moved into the 20th century, the landscape of wealth accumulation began to shift. The advent of new technologies and the rise of the information age brought forth a new breed of billionaires. Figures like Bill Gates and Steve Jobs revolutionized the tech industry, creating products and services that transformed everyday life. Their success stories inspired a generation of entrepreneurs, eager to harness the potential of emerging technologies to build their own empires.

The 21st century has seen an explosion in the number of billionaires, driven by rapid advancements in technology, globalization, and financial markets. Today's billionaires are no longer confined to traditional industries like oil and steel. They come from diverse sectors such as technology, finance, real estate, and entertainment. This diversification has led to a more interconnected and dynamic global economy, where the influence of billionaires extends across borders and industries.

Despite their immense wealth and power, modern billionaires often operate behind the scenes, exerting their influence in subtle yet profound ways. They fund political campaigns, shape public policy, and invest in groundbreaking research and development. Through their philanthropic efforts, they address pressing global challenges such as poverty, healthcare, and climate change. By leveraging their resources and networks, these silent architects continue to shape the course of history, leaving a lasting impact on the world.

2

Chapter 2: The Power of Innovation

Innovation has always been a key driver of wealth creation, and in the modern era, it has become the cornerstone of billionaire success stories. Visionaries like Elon Musk and Steve Jobs exemplify how innovation can revolutionize entire industries and create immense wealth. Musk's ventures, including Tesla and SpaceX, have not only disrupted the automotive and aerospace sectors but also spurred advancements in renewable energy and space exploration. His relentless pursuit of ambitious goals, such as colonizing Mars and transitioning the world to sustainable energy, highlights the transformative power of innovation.

Similarly, Steve Jobs' contributions to the tech industry through Apple have had a profound impact on how we interact with technology. From the introduction of the personal computer to the revolutionary iPhone, Jobs' ability to anticipate consumer needs and create products that blend functionality and design has set new standards in the industry. His legacy continues to influence the way technology companies approach innovation and product development.

The power of innovation extends beyond individual entrepreneurs to entire ecosystems. Silicon Valley, for example, has become a global hub for technological innovation, attracting talent and investment from around the world. The concentration of tech giants, startups, and venture capital in this region has created a fertile environment for new ideas to flourish. This ecosystem has produced numerous billionaires who have leveraged cutting-edge technologies to build successful companies and shape the future.

Innovation is not limited to technology; it permeates various industries, including healthcare, finance, and entertainment. Breakthroughs in biotechnology, such as gene editing and personalized medicine, have the potential to revolutionize healthcare and create new opportunities for wealth creation. In finance, the rise of fintech and blockchain technologies is reshaping the way we conduct transactions and manage assets. In entertainment, the advent of streaming services and digital content platforms has transformed how we consume media and has given rise to new billionaires who capitalize on these trends.

Ultimately, the power of innovation lies in its ability to challenge the status quo and create new possibilities. Billionaires who harness this power are not only able to amass great wealth but also drive progress and change in society. Their innovative contributions continue to shape our world, paving the way for future generations to build upon their achievements.

3

Chapter 3: Market Disruptors

Market disruptors are billionaires who revolutionize traditional industries by introducing novel business models and technologies that challenge established norms. Jeff Bezos, the founder of Amazon, is a prime example of a market disruptor who transformed the retail industry. Amazon's rise from an online bookstore to the world's largest e-commerce platform has redefined how consumers shop and how businesses operate. Bezos' relentless focus on customer satisfaction, coupled with his willingness to take risks and invest in long-term growth, has set a new standard for business innovation.

The disruption caused by Amazon extends beyond retail to various sectors, including logistics, cloud computing, and entertainment. The company's investments in logistics infrastructure have enabled faster and more efficient delivery services, setting new expectations for the industry. Amazon Web Services (AWS) has become a dominant player in the cloud computing market, providing scalable and cost-effective solutions for businesses worldwide. Additionally, Amazon's entry into the entertainment industry through Amazon Prime Video has reshaped the streaming landscape, competing with established players like Netflix and Hulu.

Other billionaires have also disrupted traditional markets in their respective industries. Elon Musk's ventures, including Tesla and SpaceX, have challenged the automotive and aerospace sectors. Tesla's electric vehicles have spurred a shift towards sustainable transportation, prompting traditional automakers to invest in electric and autonomous technologies. SpaceX's achievements in reusable rockets and space exploration have disrupted the aerospace industry, reducing the cost of space travel and opening new possibilities for commercial space ventures.

In the financial sector, fintech entrepreneurs like Jack Dorsey, the co-founder of Square, have disrupted traditional banking and payment systems. Square's innovative payment solutions have empowered small businesses and individuals to accept digital payments, challenging established financial institutions. Similarly, the rise of cryptocurrencies and blockchain technologies, spearheaded by figures like Satoshi Nakamoto, the pseudonymous creator of Bitcoin, has introduced new paradigms for decentralized finance and digital assets.

Market disruptors often face resistance from incumbents and regulatory challenges as they reshape industries. However, their ability to innovate and adapt allows them to overcome these obstacles and drive change. By challenging traditional business models and introducing new technologies, these billionaires not only create immense wealth but also redefine how industries operate and how consumers interact with products and services.

4

Chapter 4: Strategic Philanthropy

In the realm of modern billionaires, wealth is often seen as a tool for enacting positive change. Strategic philanthropy has become a hallmark of many billionaires, who leverage their resources to address global challenges. One of the most notable examples is the Bill & Melinda Gates Foundation. Established by Bill Gates, the co-founder of Microsoft, and his then-wife Melinda, this foundation has focused on improving healthcare, reducing extreme poverty, and expanding educational opportunities worldwide.

The Gates Foundation's efforts in global health have had a profound impact, particularly in the fight against infectious diseases. Through partnerships with governments, non-profits, and other organizations, the foundation has helped fund the development and distribution of vaccines for diseases such as malaria, polio, and COVID-19. Their work has saved millions of lives and demonstrated the power of strategic philanthropy to effect meaningful change.

Another prominent example of strategic philanthropy is the Giving Pledge, an initiative co-founded by Bill Gates and Warren Buffett. The Giving Pledge encourages billionaires to commit the majority of their wealth to philanthropic causes, either during their lifetimes or in their wills. By inspiring a culture of giving among the world's wealthiest individuals, the pledge aims to address a wide range of social and environmental issues, from poverty and education to climate change and scientific research.

Philanthropy is not limited to financial contributions; it also involves leveraging expertise, networks, and influence to drive progress. For instance, Elon Musk's efforts to advance renewable energy and space exploration are not only driven by profit but also by a desire to address critical challenges facing humanity. Musk's ventures, such as Tesla's electric vehicles and SpaceX's reusable rockets, are aligned with his vision of a sustainable and multi-planetary future.

Strategic philanthropy is not without its criticisms. Some argue that billionaire philanthropy can perpetuate existing power structures and divert attention from systemic issues that require collective action. Critics also point to the potential for philanthropic efforts to reflect the personal priorities and biases of the donors, rather than addressing the most pressing needs of society. Nonetheless, the contributions of billionaire philanthropists continue to play a significant role in addressing global challenges and shaping the future.

5

Chapter 5: Media Moguls and Influence

Media ownership has long been a powerful tool for shaping public opinion and influencing political discourse. Billionaires who control major media outlets wield significant influence over the information that reaches the public. Rupert Murdoch, the founder of News Corp, is a prime example of a media mogul whose empire spans television, newspapers, and online platforms. Murdoch's influence extends across continents, with prominent media holdings in the United States, the United Kingdom, and Australia.

Through his ownership of media outlets such as Fox News, The Wall Street Journal, and The Times, Murdoch has been able to shape public narratives and influence political agendas. Fox News, in particular, has become a dominant force in American cable news, known for its conservative perspective and its impact on the political landscape. Murdoch's media empire exemplifies how billionaires can use their control of information to shape public opinion and drive political discourse.

Other billionaires have also made significant investments in media to amplify their influence. Jeff Bezos, the founder of Amazon, acquired The Washington Post in 2013. Under Bezos' ownership, the newspaper has expanded its digital presence and enhanced its investigative reporting capabilities. The Washington Post's coverage of political and social issues has garnered widespread attention and influenced public debate.

In the digital age, media influence extends beyond traditional print and broadcast outlets to social media and online platforms. Mark Zuckerberg, the co-founder of Facebook, has built one of the most influential digital platforms in the world. With billions of users, Facebook plays a central role in the dissemination of information, shaping public discourse, and connecting people globally. The platform's algorithms and policies have a profound impact on the visibility and spread of content, raising questions about the responsibilities of tech billionaires in managing the flow of information.

The influence of media moguls is not without controversy. Concerns about media bias, monopolistic practices, and the concentration of media ownership have led to calls for greater transparency and regulation. Critics argue that the power wielded by media billionaires can undermine democratic processes and distort public perceptions. Despite these challenges, the role of media moguls in shaping information and influence remains a defining feature of the modern billionaire landscape.

6

Chapter 6: Financial Titans

In the world of finance, certain billionaires have emerged as titans, wielding immense influence over global markets and economies. Hedge fund managers, private equity magnates, and investment bankers are among the financial elite who have amassed vast fortunes through strategic investments and financial acumen. One of the most prominent figures in this realm is George Soros, the founder of Soros Fund Management and the Open Society Foundations.

Soros is renowned for his success as a hedge fund manager, particularly for his bold and profitable currency trades. His most famous trade, known as "breaking the Bank of England," involved shorting the British pound in 1992, resulting in significant profits and earning him a reputation as one of the most astute investors in history. Beyond his financial achievements, Soros has been a vocal advocate for open societies, using his wealth to support democratic governance, human rights, and education through the Open Society Foundations.

Private equity magnates, such as Stephen Schwarzman of Blackstone Group, have also left an indelible mark on the financial landscape. Blackstone's investments span various industries, including real estate, technology, and healthcare. Schwarzman's leadership has transformed Blackstone into one of the world's largest private equity firms, with assets under management totaling hundreds of billions of dollars. The firm's investments and acquisitions have reshaped entire sectors, demonstrating the transformative power of private equity.

Investment bankers, such as Lloyd Blankfein, the former CEO of Goldman Sachs, have played a pivotal role in shaping financial markets and advising corporations on mergers, acquisitions, and capital raising. Goldman Sachs' influence extends across global markets, with its investment banking, asset management, and securities divisions driving financial innovation and economic growth. The bank's involvement in major financial transactions and its role in navigating economic crises highlight the influence of investment banking billionaires.

The financial titans wield considerable power, but their actions also attract scrutiny and criticism. Concerns about income inequality, market manipulation, and the influence of finance on politics have sparked debates about the ethical responsibilities of financial billionaires. Regulatory reforms and calls for greater transparency aim to address these challenges and ensure that the influence of financial titans benefits society as a whole.

7

Chapter 7: The Real Estate Emperors

Real estate has long been a significant avenue for wealth creation, and many billionaires have amassed their fortunes through strategic investments in property. Donald Trump, a real estate mogul turned politician, is one of the most recognizable figures in this realm. Trump's real estate empire, which includes iconic properties such as Trump Tower in New York City and luxury resorts around the world, showcases the potential for significant returns in the real estate market.

Real estate billionaires often invest in prime locations and develop high-end properties that cater to affluent clientele. These investments not only generate substantial income but also influence urban landscapes and real estate trends. For instance, the developments led by Sheldon Adelson, the founder of Las Vegas Sands Corporation, have transformed the Las Vegas Strip into a premier destination for luxury hotels and casinos. Adelson's investments in integrated resorts have reshaped the hospitality and entertainment industries, attracting millions of visitors annually.

Beyond commercial real estate, residential properties also offer lucrative opportunities for wealth creation. Billionaires like Jeff Greene and Sam Zell have made their fortunes through residential real estate investments, including rental properties, condominiums, and housing developments. Their portfolios span multiple cities and countries, highlighting the global nature of real estate investments.

The impact of real estate billionaires extends beyond individual properties to entire communities and cities. Their investments can drive economic growth, create jobs, and enhance infrastructure. For example, the urban renewal projects spearheaded by billionaires like Stephen Ross, the chairman of Related Companies, have revitalized neighborhoods and contributed to the development of modern, sustainable urban environments. Ross' Hudson Yards development in New York City is one of the largest real estate projects in U.S. history, featuring commercial, residential, and cultural spaces that attract businesses and residents alike.

However, the influence of real estate billionaires is not without controversy. Concerns about gentrification, housing affordability, and the environmental impact of large-scale developments have sparked debates about the ethical responsibilities of real estate investors. As urbanization continues to shape the future, the role of real estate billionaires in balancing profit with social and environmental considerations remains a critical issue.

8

Chapter 8: Political Power Players

The intersection of wealth and politics has long been a source of intrigue and controversy. Billionaires often use their financial resources and influence to shape political outcomes and public policy. Michael Bloomberg, the founder of Bloomberg LP and former mayor of New York City, exemplifies the political power player who leverages wealth for political engagement. Bloomberg's substantial financial contributions to political campaigns and advocacy groups have made him a prominent figure in U.S. politics.

Bloomberg's tenure as mayor of New York City saw significant initiatives in public health, education, and urban development. His philanthropic efforts, including the Bloomberg Philanthropies, have supported various causes, from climate change to gun control. Bloomberg's presidential campaign in 2020, funded primarily by his own wealth, demonstrated the potential for billionaires to influence electoral politics and policy debates.

Other billionaires have also wielded political influence through campaign contributions, lobbying, and advocacy. The Koch brothers, Charles and David Koch, have been influential in shaping conservative political agendas in the United States. Through their funding of think tanks, advocacy groups, and political candidates, the Kochs have promoted policies aligned with their libertarian and free-market principles. Their contributions have had a lasting impact on American politics and public policy.

In addition to direct political engagement, billionaires often use their media ownership to shape political discourse and public opinion. As mentioned in Chapter 5, media moguls like Rupert Murdoch and Jeff Bezos have the power to influence political narratives through their control of major news outlets. This influence can extend to shaping public perceptions, framing policy debates, and supporting political candidates.

The involvement of billionaires in politics raises questions about the balance of power and the role of money in democracy. Critics argue that the concentration of wealth and political influence in the hands of a few individuals undermines democratic principles and exacerbates inequality. Calls for campaign finance reform and greater transparency aim to address these concerns and ensure that political power is more equitably distributed.

9

Chapter 9: Global Expansion

In today's interconnected world, billionaires often extend their influence beyond national borders, pursuing global expansion to reach new markets and opportunities. Jack Ma, the founder of Alibaba Group, is a prime example of a billionaire who has achieved remarkable success through international growth. Alibaba's e-commerce platforms, including Taobao and Tmall, have revolutionized online shopping in China and expanded to serve millions of customers worldwide.

Ma's vision for Alibaba extends beyond e-commerce to encompass cloud computing, digital payments, and entertainment. The company's global expansion has included partnerships, acquisitions, and investments in various countries, reflecting its ambition to become a global technology powerhouse. Alibaba's influence on global trade and the digital economy highlights the potential for billionaires to drive international business growth and innovation.

Similarly, other billionaires have pursued global expansion to tap into emerging markets and diversify their investments. Mukesh Ambani, the chairman of Reliance Industries, has expanded his conglomerate's presence in sectors such as telecommunications, retail, and energy. Reliance's Jio platform has transformed India's digital landscape, providing affordable internet access to millions of people and fostering digital inclusion. Ambani's investments in renewable energy and technology further underscore his commitment to global growth and sustainability.

The global reach of billionaires is not limited to business ventures; it also extends to philanthropy and social impact. Philanthropists like George Soros and Bill Gates have supported international initiatives to address global challenges, from public health to education. Their efforts have contributed to the advancement of scientific research, the eradication of diseases, and the promotion of human rights worldwide.

Global expansion also involves navigating complex regulatory environments, cultural differences, and geopolitical dynamics. Billionaires who successfully expand their influence internationally must balance local and global considerations, adapting their strategies to diverse markets and contexts. The ability to operate effectively on a global scale underscores the strategic acumen and vision of these modern titans.

10

Chapter 10: Tech Giants and the Future

The technology sector has produced some of the most influential and visionary billionaires of our time. Tech giants like Mark Zuckerberg, the co-founder of Facebook, have reshaped the digital landscape and transformed how we connect, communicate, and consume information. Facebook's social media platforms, including Instagram and WhatsApp, have billions of users worldwide, making it one of the most powerful digital ecosystems in existence.

Zuckerberg's vision for Facebook extends beyond social networking to encompass virtual reality, artificial intelligence, and the metaverse. The company's investments in Oculus VR and its rebranding as Meta reflect its commitment to pioneering new digital frontiers. By pushing the boundaries of technology, Zuckerberg aims to create immersive and interconnected virtual experiences that redefine the way we interact with the digital world.

Other tech billionaires, such as Larry Page and Sergey Brin, the co-founders of Google, have also had a profound impact on the digital age. Google's search engine, cloud services, and innovations in artificial intelligence have revolutionized how we access and process information. The company's ventures into autonomous vehicles, smart devices, and quantum computing demonstrate its commitment to shaping the future of technology.

Elon Musk's ventures, including SpaceX and Neuralink, represent bold visions for the future. SpaceX's achievements in reusable rockets and space exploration have paved the way for commercial space travel and the potential colonization of Mars. Neuralink's research into brain-computer interfaces aims to enhance human cognition and address neurological disorders. Musk's ambitious goals reflect the transformative potential of technology to address some of humanity's most pressing challenges.

The influence of tech giants extends beyond their products and services; it also shapes societal norms and values. The ethical considerations of technology, including data privacy, artificial intelligence, and the digital divide, are critical issues that tech billionaires must navigate. As technology continues to advance at a rapid pace, the role of tech giants in shaping the future will be paramount, with their innovations driving progress and shaping the trajectory of human civilization.

The Silent Architects: How Billionaires Shape Industries, Redraw Maps, and Rewrite History

In a world where wealth wields unprecedented influence, a select few individuals stand as the silent architects of our time. These modern titans, often shrouded in mystery, shape entire industries, redraw national boundaries, and leave indelible marks on history. "The Silent Architects" takes readers on a riveting journey through the lives and legacies of the world's most powerful billionaires.

From the rise of tech giants like Elon Musk and Mark Zuckerberg to the strategic philanthropy of Bill Gates, this book uncovers the intricate web of innovation, ambition, and influence that defines today's billionaires. Through compelling narratives and in-depth analysis, discover how visionaries like Jeff Bezos transformed retail with Amazon, and how media moguls like Rupert Murdoch shape public opinion and politics.

Explore the disruptive forces that revolutionize traditional markets, the real estate emperors who reshape urban landscapes, and the financial titans whose investments drive global economies. Delve into the global expansion strategies of entrepreneurs like Jack Ma and the future-focused innovations of tech giants that redefine our digital age.

"The Silent Architects" also examines the ethical dilemmas and societal impacts of immense wealth. With thought-provoking insights and captivating stories, this book offers a nuanced perspective on the billionaires who, often behind the scenes, mold the world as we know it.

Join us in unraveling the secrets of these silent architects and understanding the profound ways they shape industries, redraw maps, and rewrite history.

www.ingramcontent.com/pod-product-compliance
Lightning Source LLC
LaVergne TN
LVHW020509080526
838202LV00057B/6253